The Over-thinker's Journal

A DAY BY DAY GUIDE FOR
THOSE OF US WHOSE
MINDS NEVER REST.

Hello my friend!

First thing's first- you are amazing. Just the fact that you've picked this journal up and made it onto the second page shows that you are trying to take care of yourself. Self-love can be damn hard to stick with, especially when our lives are full of expectations we feel we can't live up to.

A little bit about myself. I've struggled with anxiety and depression for as long as I can remember. Constantly battling with how I think I should be and how I actually am. Always feeling as though I am not good enough, not smart enough, not strong enough, not brave enough. However around 5 years ago I also developed Myalgic Encephalopathy (CFS/ME), which, let me tell you, absolutely sucks! My expectations of myself are ridiculous and completely irrational and and I know that and yet, I still have them.

I've designed this journal with people just like me (and I assume you!) in mind. People whose brains are full of thoughts that are hard to keep tabs on. People who need to be reminded that just getting through the day is sometimes a big achievement. People who judge themselves too harshly and need to learn to love themselves more. People who expect so much from themselves-expectations they wouldn't put on anyone else. People who struggle.

My hope is that this journal will help you to organise your thoughts, feelings, needs and wants. It is split into weekly sections, each containing a mental health tracker, a habit tracker, daily pages and weekly mind dumps along with positive phrases and distraction pages for when things are particularly rough. Use what you want, leave what you don't want. Write in pretty colours, use the same blunt pencil. Make every page gorgeous, scribble notes all over the place. It's your journal and so what you do with it is completely up to you.

Just remember:
You ARE good enough,
You ARE smart enough,
You ARE strong enough,
and you ARE brave enough.

- Attila Made

xx

THE NUMBER 1 SKILL IN LIFE IS NOT GIVING UP

MENTAL HEALTH

WEEK 1 :_____

DAY 1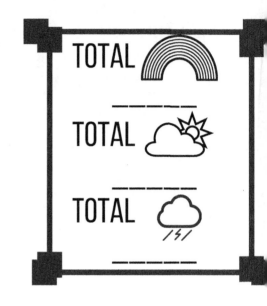

DAY 2

DAY 3

DAY 4

DAY 5

DAY 6

DAY 7

TOTAL

_____

TOTAL

_____

TOTAL

_____

BEST DAY

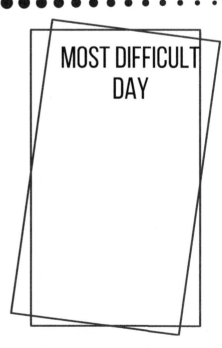

MOST DIFFICULT DAY

HABIT TRACKER

WEEK 1: _____

HABIT	GOAL	1	2	3	4	5	6	7	CHANGES TO MAKE

DAY 1:_____

MY PLANS

MY GOALS

MY ACHIEVEMENTS

MY WORRIES

MY FAVOURITE MOMENT

MY MIND

DAY 2:_____

MY PLANS

MY GOALS

MY ACHIEVEMENTS

MY WORRIES

MY FAVOURITE MOMENT

MY MIND

DAY 3:_____

MY PLANS

MY GOALS

MY ACHIEVEMENTS

MY WORRIES

MY FAVOURITE MOMENT

MY MIND

DAY 4:_____

MY PLANS

MY GOALS

MY ACHIEVEMENTS

MY WORRIES

MY FAVOURITE MOMENT

MY MIND

DAY 5:_____

MY PLANS

MY GOALS

MY ACHIEVEMENTS

MY WORRIES

MY FAVOURITE MOMENT

MY MIND

DAY 6:_____

MY PLANS

MY GOALS

MY ACHIEVEMENTS

MY WORRIES

MY FAVOURITE MOMENT

MY MIND

DAY 7:_____

MY PLANS

MY GOALS

MY ACHIEVEMENTS

MY WORRIES

MY FAVOURITE MOMENT

MY MIND

WORK HARD, DREAM BIG.

WEEK 1 MIND DUMP

MENTAL HEALTH

WEEK 2 :_____

DAY 1

DAY 2

DAY 3

DAY 4

DAY 5

DAY 6

DAY 7

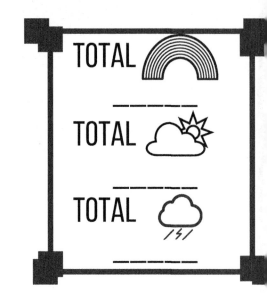

TOTAL

_____

TOTAL

_____

TOTAL

_____

BEST DAY

MOST DIFFICULT DAY

HABIT TRACKER

WEEK 2 : _____

HABIT	GOAL	1	2	3	4	5	6	7	CHANGES TO MAKE

DAY 1:_____

MY PLANS

MY GOALS

MY ACHIEVEMENTS

MY WORRIES

MY FAVOURITE MOMENT

MY MIND

DAY 2:_____

MY PLANS

MY GOALS

MY ACHIEVEMENTS

MY WORRIES

MY FAVOURITE MOMENT

MY MIND

DAY 3:_____

MY PLANS

MY GOALS

MY ACHIEVEMENTS

MY WORRIES

MY FAVOURITE MOMENT

MY MIND

DAY 4:_____

MY PLANS

MY GOALS

MY ACHIEVEMENTS

MY WORRIES

MY FAVOURITE MOMENT

MY MIND

DAY 5:_____

MY PLANS

MY GOALS

MY ACHIEVEMENTS

MY WORRIES

MY FAVOURITE MOMENT

MY MIND

DAY 6:_____

MY PLANS

MY GOALS

MY ACHIEVEMENTS

MY WORRIES

MY FAVOURITE MOMENT

MY MIND

DAY 7:_____

MY PLANS

MY GOALS

MY ACHIEVEMENTS

MY WORRIES

MY FAVOURITE MOMENT

MY MIND

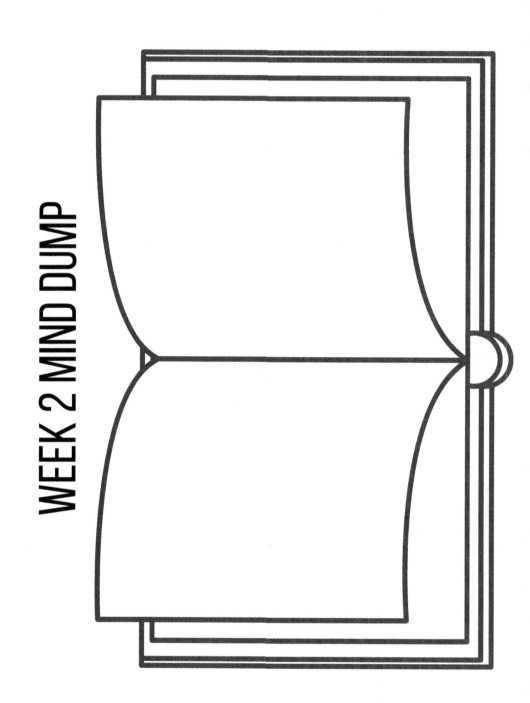

WEEK 2 MIND DUMP

DON'T RUSH SOMETHING YOU WANT TO LAST FOREUER

MENTAL HEALTH

WEEK 3 :_____

DAY 1
DAY 2
DAY 3
DAY 4
DAY 5
DAY 6
DAY 7

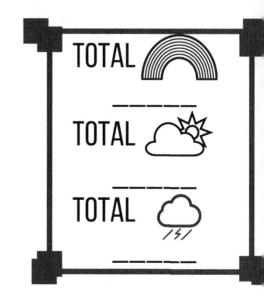

TOTAL _____

TOTAL _____

TOTAL _____

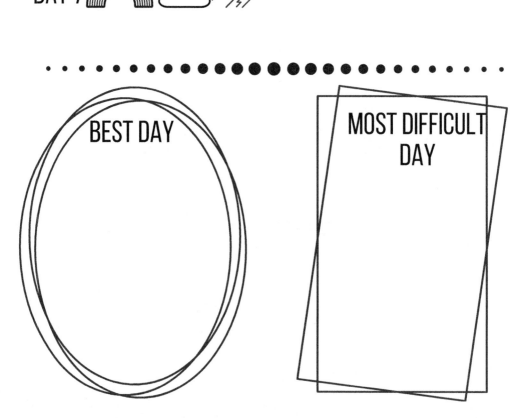

BEST DAY

MOST DIFFICULT DAY

HABIT TRACKER

WEEK 3 :_____

HABIT	GOAL	1	2	3	4	5	6	7	CHANGES TO MAKE

DAY 1:_____

MY PLANS

MY GOALS

MY ACHIEVEMENTS

MY WORRIES

MY FAVOURITE MOMENT

MY MIND

DAY 2:_____

MY PLANS

MY GOALS

MY ACHIEVEMENTS

MY WORRIES

MY FAVOURITE MOMENT

MY MIND

DAY 3:_____

MY PLANS

MY GOALS

MY ACHIEVEMENTS

MY WORRIES

MY FAVOURITE MOMENT

MY MIND

DAY 4:_____

MY PLANS

MY GOALS

MY ACHIEVEMENTS

MY WORRIES

MY FAVOURITE MOMENT

MY MIND

DAY 5:_____

MY PLANS

MY GOALS

MY ACHIEVEMENTS

MY WORRIES

MY FAVOURITE MOMENT

MY MIND

DAY 6:_____

MY PLANS

MY GOALS

MY ACHIEVEMENTS

MY WORRIES

MY FAVOURITE MOMENT

MY MIND

DAY 7:_____

MY PLANS

MY GOALS

MY ACHIEVEMENTS

MY WORRIES

MY FAVOURITE MOMENT

MY MIND

WEEK 3 MIND DUMP

MENTAL HEALTH

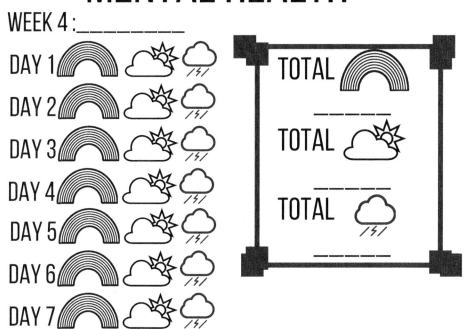

WEEK 4 :_____

DAY 1
DAY 2
DAY 3
DAY 4
DAY 5
DAY 6
DAY 7

TOTAL _____

TOTAL _____

TOTAL _____

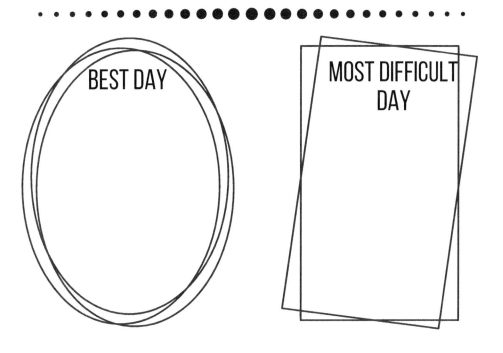

BEST DAY

MOST DIFFICULT DAY

HABIT TRACKER

WEEK 4: _____

HABIT	GOAL	1	2	3	4	5	6	7	CHANGES TO MAKE

Repeat after me ...
I can do this!

DAY 1:_____

MY PLANS

MY GOALS

MY ACHIEVEMENTS

MY WORRIES

MY FAVOURITE MOMENT

MY MIND

DAY 2:_____

MY PLANS

MY GOALS

MY ACHIEVEMENTS

MY WORRIES

MY FAVOURITE MOMENT

MY MIND

DAY 3:_____

MY PLANS

MY GOALS

MY ACHIEVEMENTS

MY WORRIES

MY FAVOURITE MOMENT

MY MIND

DAY 4:_____

MY PLANS

MY GOALS

MY ACHIEVEMENTS

MY WORRIES

MY FAVOURITE MOMENT

MY MIND

DAY 5:_____

MY PLANS

MY GOALS

MY ACHIEVEMENTS

MY WORRIES

MY FAVOURITE MOMENT

MY MIND

DAY 6:_____

MY PLANS

MY GOALS

MY ACHIEVEMENTS

MY WORRIES

MY FAVOURITE MOMENT

MY MIND

DAY 7:_____

MY PLANS

MY GOALS

MY ACHIEVEMENTS

MY WORRIES

MY FAVOURITE MOMENT

MY MIND

WEEK 4 MIND DUMP

MENTAL HEALTH

WEEK 5 :_____

DAY 1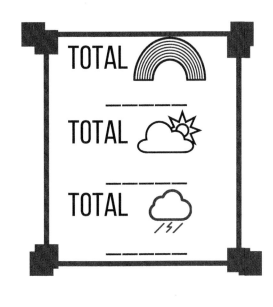

DAY 2

DAY 3

DAY 4

DAY 5

DAY 6

DAY 7

TOTAL

_____

TOTAL

_____

TOTAL

_____

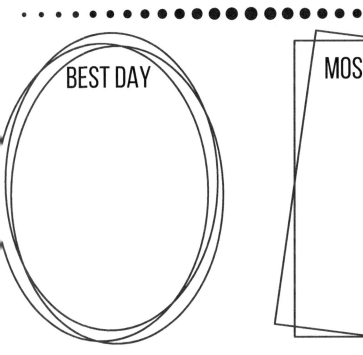

BEST DAY

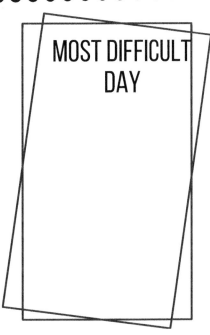

MOST DIFFICULT DAY

HABIT TRACKER

WEEK 5: _____

HABIT	GOAL	1	2	3	4	5	6	7	CHANGES TO MAKE

DAY 1:_____

MY PLANS

MY GOALS

MY ACHIEVEMENTS

MY WORRIES

MY FAVOURITE MOMENT

MY MIND

DAY 2:_____

MY PLANS

MY GOALS

MY ACHIEVEMENTS

MY WORRIES

MY FAVOURITE MOMENT

MY MIND

DAY 3:_____

MY PLANS

MY GOALS

MY ACHIEVEMENTS

MY WORRIES

MY FAVOURITE MOMENT

MY MIND

DAY 4:_____

MY PLANS

MY GOALS

MY ACHIEVEMENTS

MY WORRIES

MY FAVOURITE MOMENT

MY MIND

DAY 5:_____

MY PLANS

MY GOALS

MY ACHIEVEMENTS

MY WORRIES

MY FAVOURITE MOMENT

MY MIND

DAY 6:_____

MY PLANS

MY GOALS

MY ACHIEVEMENTS

MY WORRIES

MY FAVOURITE MOMENT

MY MIND

TAKE A DEEP BREATH. IT'S A BAD DAY NOT A BAD LIFE.

DAY 7:_____

MY PLANS

MY GOALS

MY ACHIEVEMENTS

MY WORRIES

MY FAVOURITE MOMENT

MY MIND

WEEK 5 MIND DUMP

MENTAL HEALTH

WEEK 6 : _____

DAY 1
DAY 2
DAY 3
DAY 4
DAY 5
DAY 6
DAY 7

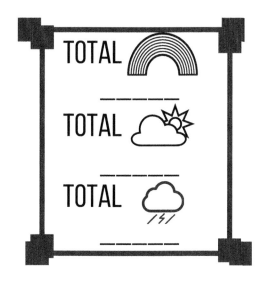

TOTAL _____

TOTAL _____

TOTAL _____

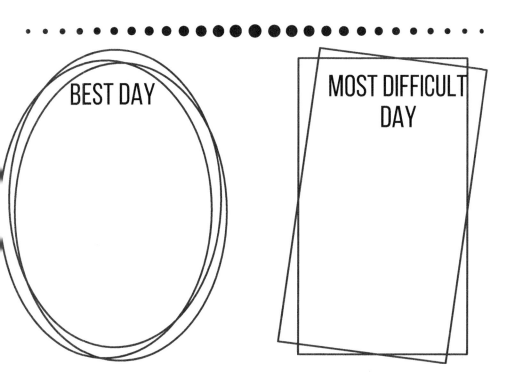

BEST DAY

MOST DIFFICULT DAY

WEEK 6: _____ HABIT TRACKER

HABIT	GOAL	1	2	3	4	5	6	7	CHANGES TO MAKE

DAY 1:_____

MY PLANS

MY GOALS

MY ACHIEVEMENTS

MY WORRIES

MY FAVOURITE MOMENT

MY MIND

DAY 2:_____

MY PLANS

MY GOALS

MY ACHIEVEMENTS

MY WORRIES

MY FAVOURITE MOMENT

MY MIND

DAY 3:_____

MY PLANS

MY GOALS

MY ACHIEVEMENTS

MY WORRIES

MY FAVOURITE MOMENT

MY MIND

DAY 4:_____

MY PLANS

MY GOALS

MY ACHIEVEMENTS

MY WORRIES

MY FAVOURITE MOMENT

MY MIND

DAY 5:_____

MY PLANS

MY GOALS

MY ACHIEVEMENTS

MY WORRIES

MY FAVOURITE MOMENT

MY MIND

DAY 6:_____

MY PLANS

MY GOALS

MY ACHIEVEMENTS

MY WORRIES

MY FAVOURITE MOMENT

MY MIND

DAY 7:_____

MY PLANS

MY GOALS

MY ACHIEVEMENTS

MY WORRIES

MY FAVOURITE MOMENT

MY MIND

WEEK 6 MIND DUMP

MENTAL HEALTH

WEEK 7 :_____

DAY 1
DAY 2
DAY 3
DAY 4
DAY 5
DAY 6
DAY 7

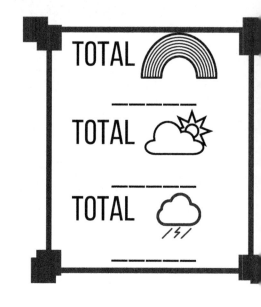

TOTAL _____

TOTAL _____

TOTAL _____

BEST DAY

MOST DIFFICULT DAY

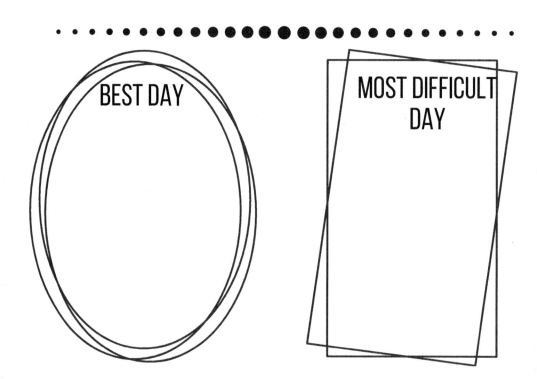

HABIT TRACKER

WEEK 7 : _____

HABIT	GOAL	1	2	3	4	5	6	7	CHANGES TO MAKE

DAY 1:_____

MY PLANS

MY GOALS

MY ACHIEVEMENTS

MY WORRIES

MY FAVOURITE MOMENT

MY MIND

DAY 2:_____

MY PLANS

MY GOALS

MY ACHIEVEMENTS

MY WORRIES

MY FAVOURITE MOMENT

MY MIND

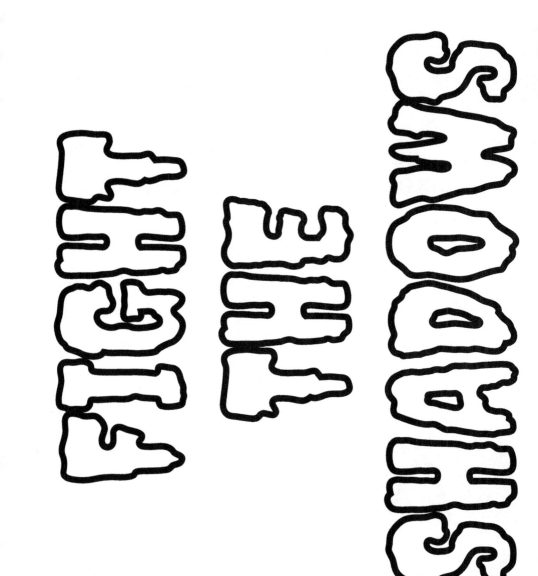

DAY 3:_____

MY PLANS

MY GOALS

MY ACHIEVEMENTS

MY WORRIES

MY FAVOURITE MOMENT

MY MIND

DAY 4:_____

MY PLANS

MY GOALS

MY ACHIEVEMENTS

MY WORRIES

MY FAVOURITE MOMENT

MY MIND

DAY 5:_____

MY PLANS

MY GOALS

MY ACHIEVEMENTS

MY WORRIES

MY FAVOURITE MOMENT

MY MIND

```
++++++++++++++++++++++++++++++++++++++++++++++++++++++++
1111111111111111111111111111111111111111111111111111111
1111111111111111111111111111111111111111111111111111111
1111111111111111111111111111111111111111111111111111111
1111111111111111111111111111111111111111111111111111111
11111111111111111111111111111111111111111I111111111111
1111111111111111111111111111111111111111111111111111111
1111111111111111111111111111111111111111111111111111111
```

```
OOOOOOOOOOOOOOOOOOOOOOOOOOOOOOOOOOOOOOOOOOOOOOOOOO
OOOOOOOOOOOOOOOOOOOOOOOOOOOOOOOOOOOOOOOOOOOOOOOOOO
OOOOOOOO0OOOOOOOOOOOOOOOOOOOOOOOOOOOOOOOOOOOOOOOOO
OOOOOOOOOOOOOOOOOOOOOOOOOOOOOOOOOOOOOOOOOOOOOOOOOO
OOOOOOOOOOOOOOOOOOOOOOOOOOOOOOOOOOOOOOOOOOOOOOOOOO
OOOOOOOOOOOOOOOOOOOOOOOOOOOOOOOOOOOOOOOOOOOOOOOOOO
OOOOOOOOOOOOOOOOOOOOOOOOOOOOOOOOOOOOOOOOOOOOOOOOOO
OOOOOOOOOOOOOOOOOOOOOOOOOOOOOOOOOOOOOOOOOOOOOOOOOO
```

```
OOOOOOOOOOOOOOOOOOOOOOOOOOOOOOOOOOOOOOOOOOOOOOOOOOO
OOOOOOOOOOOOOOOOOOOOOOOOOOOOOOOOOOOOOOOOOOOOOOOOOOO
OOOOOOOOOOOOOOOOOOOOOOOOOOOOOOOOOOOOOOOOOOOOOOOQO
OOOOOOOOOOOOOOOOOOOOOOOOOOOOOOOOOOOOOOOOOOOOOOOOOOO
OOOOOOOOOOOOOOOOOOOOOOOOOOOOOOOOOOOOOOOOOOOOOOOOOOO
OOOOOOOOOOOOOOOOOOOOOOOOOOOOOOOOOOOOOOOOOOOOOOOOOOO
OOOOOOOOOOOOOOOOOOOOOOOOOOOOOOOOOOOOOOOOOOOOOOOOOOO
OOOOOOOOOOOOOOOOOOOOOOOOOOOOOOOOOOOOOOOOOOOOOOOOOOO
```

DAY 6:_____

MY PLANS

MY GOALS

MY ACHIEVEMENTS

MY WORRIES

MY FAVOURITE MOMENT

MY MIND

DAY 7:_____

MY PLANS

MY GOALS

MY ACHIEVEMENTS

MY WORRIES

MY FAVOURITE MOMENT

MY MIND

WEEK 7 MIND DUMP

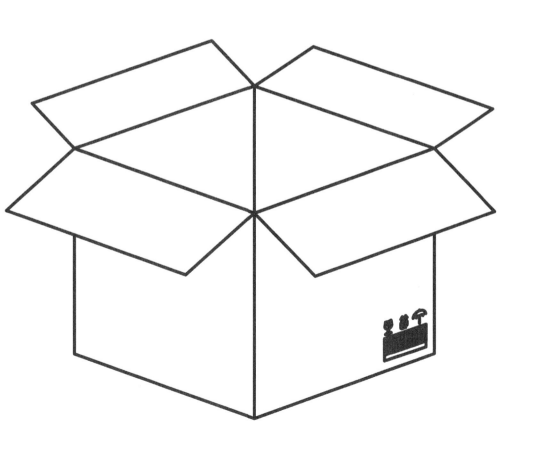

MENTAL HEALTH

WEEK 8 :_____

DAY 1

DAY 2

DAY 3

DAY 4

DAY 5

DAY 6

DAY 7

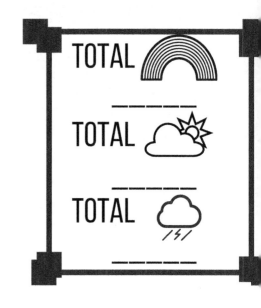

TOTAL _____

TOTAL _____

TOTAL _____

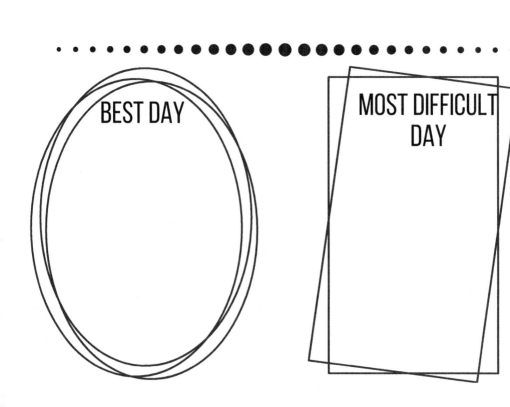

BEST DAY

MOST DIFFICULT DAY

HABIT TRACKER

WEEK 8 :_____

HABIT	GOAL	1	2	3	4	5	6	7	CHANGES TO MAKE

DAY 1:_____

MY PLANS

MY GOALS

MY ACHIEVEMENTS

MY WORRIES

MY FAVOURITE MOMENT

MY MIND

DAY 2:_____

MY PLANS

MY GOALS

MY ACHIEVEMENTS

MY WORRIES

MY FAVOURITE MOMENT

MY MIND

DAY 3:_____

MY PLANS

MY GOALS

MY ACHIEVEMENTS

MY WORRIES

MY FAVOURITE MOMENT

MY MIND

DAY 4:_____

MY PLANS

MY GOALS

MY ACHIEVEMENTS

MY WORRIES

MY FAVOURITE MOMENT

MY MIND

DAY 5:_____

MY PLANS

MY GOALS

MY ACHIEVEMENTS

MY WORRIES

MY FAVOURITE MOMENT

MY MIND

DAY 6:_____

MY PLANS

MY GOALS

MY ACHIEVEMENTS

MY WORRIES

MY FAVOURITE MOMENT

MY MIND

DAY 7:_____

MY PLANS

MY GOALS

MY ACHIEVEMENTS

MY WORRIES

MY FAVOURITE MOMENT

MY MIND

WEEK 8 MIND DUMP

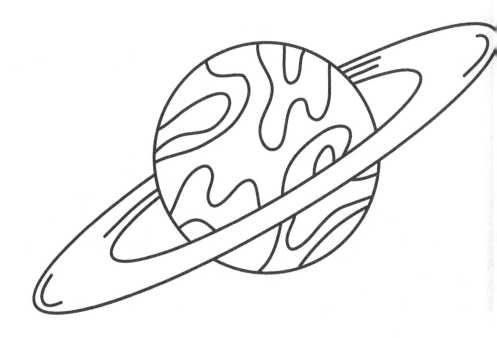

Hello my friend!

If you've made it to this page it means you are now half way through the journal- amazing stuff! Take this time to truly think about how the last two months have been for you.

Are you having more rainbow days, or cloud or storm days at the moment?

Have your habits goals been realistic, or unattainable?

Have any days been just utterly incredible? What happened?

Have there been any days that have felt too hard? What happened?

What are you most proud of achieving over the last two months?

What do you hope to achieve over the next two months?

Sometimes we screw up. Sometimes we feel that we let ourselves or others down. Sometimes we 'just can't. And that is all ok. I am so proud of you for everything you have done so far. Whether you've met every habit goal and had all rainbow days, or even the most basic of habits has been too much and your days are full of worries and storms, the fact that you are trying is the most important thing.

Remember, failing is ok, giving up is not.

- Attila Made

xx

MENTAL HEALTH

WEEK 9 : _____

DAY 1
DAY 2
DAY 3
DAY 4
DAY 5
DAY 6
DAY 7

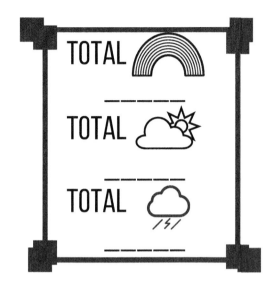

TOTAL _____

TOTAL _____

TOTAL _____

BEST DAY

MOST DIFFICULT DAY

WEEK 9 : _____

HABIT TRACKER

HABIT	GOAL	1	2	3	4	5	6	7	CHANGES TO MAKE

DAY 1:_____

MY PLANS

MY GOALS

MY ACHIEVEMENTS

MY WORRIES

MY FAVOURITE MOMENT

MY MIND

DAY 2:_____

MY PLANS

MY GOALS

MY ACHIEVEMENTS

MY WORRIES

MY FAVOURITE MOMENT

MY MIND

DAY 3:_____

MY PLANS

MY GOALS

MY ACHIEVEMENTS

MY WORRIES

MY FAVOURITE MOMENT

MY MIND

DAY 4:_____

MY PLANS

MY GOALS

MY ACHIEVEMENTS

MY WORRIES

MY FAVOURITE MOMENT

MY MIND

It doesn't get easier, you get stronger.

DAY 5:_____

MY PLANS

MY GOALS

MY ACHIEVEMENTS

MY WORRIES

MY FAVOURITE MOMENT

MY MIND

DAY 6:_____

MY PLANS

MY GOALS

MY ACHIEVEMENTS

MY WORRIES

MY FAVOURITE MOMENT

MY MIND

DAY 7:_____

MY PLANS

MY GOALS

MY ACHIEVEMENTS

MY WORRIES

MY FAVOURITE MOMENT

MY MIND

WEEK 9 MIND DUMP

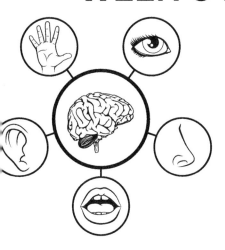

MENTAL HEALTH

WEEK 10 :_____

DAY 1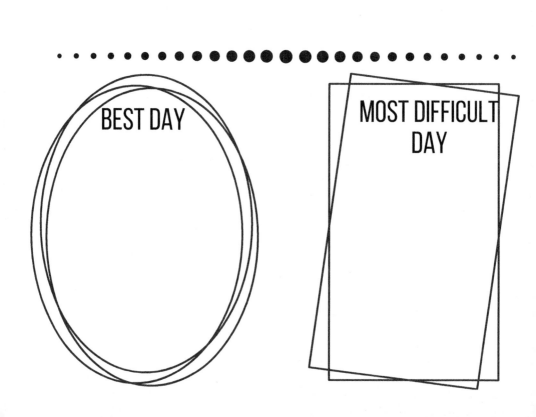

DAY 2

DAY 3

DAY 4

DAY 5

DAY 6

DAY 7

TOTAL

_____

TOTAL

_____

TOTAL

_____

BEST DAY

MOST DIFFICULT DAY

HABIT TRACKER

WEEK 10 : _____

HABIT	GOAL	1	2	3	4	5	6	7	CHANGES TO MAKE

DAY 1:_____

MY PLANS

MY GOALS

MY ACHIEVEMENTS

MY WORRIES

MY FAVOURITE MOMENT

MY MIND

DAY 2:_____

MY PLANS

MY GOALS

MY ACHIEVEMENTS

MY WORRIES

MY FAVOURITE MOMENT

MY MIND

DAY 3:_____

MY PLANS

MY GOALS

MY ACHIEVEMENTS

MY WORRIES

MY FAVOURITE MOMENT

MY MIND

DAY 4:_____

MY PLANS

MY GOALS

MY ACHIEVEMENTS

MY WORRIES

MY FAVOURITE MOMENT

MY MIND

DAY 5:_____

MY PLANS

MY GOALS

MY ACHIEVEMENTS

MY WORRIES

MY FAVOURITE MOMENT

MY MIND

DAY 6:_____

MY PLANS

MY GOALS

MY ACHIEVEMENTS

MY WORRIES

MY FAVOURITE MOMENT

MY MIND

DAY 7:_____

MY PLANS

MY GOALS

MY ACHIEVEMENTS

MY WORRIES

MY FAVOURITE MOMENT

MY MIND

THE VOICE THAT SAYS YOU CAN'T DO IT?

IT'S A LIAR.

WEEK 10 MIND DUMP

MENTAL HEALTH

WEEK 11 : _____

DAY 1

DAY 2

DAY 3

DAY 4

DAY 5

DAY 6

DAY 7

TOTAL

_____

TOTAL

_____

TOTAL

_____

BEST DAY

MOST DIFFICULT DAY

HABIT TRACKER

WEEK 11: _____

HABIT	GOAL	1	2	3	4	5	6	7	CHANGES TO MAKE

DAY 1:_____

MY PLANS

MY GOALS

MY ACHIEVEMENTS

MY WORRIES

MY FAVOURITE MOMENT

MY MIND

DAY 2:_____

MY PLANS

MY GOALS

MY ACHIEVEMENTS

MY WORRIES

MY FAVOURITE MOMENT

MY MIND

DAY 3:_____

MY PLANS

MY GOALS

MY ACHIEVEMENTS

MY WORRIES

MY FAVOURITE MOMENT

MY MIND

DAY 4:_____

MY PLANS

MY GOALS

MY ACHIEVEMENTS

MY WORRIES

MY FAVOURITE MOMENT

MY MIND

DAY 5:_____

MY PLANS

MY GOALS

MY ACHIEVEMENTS

MY WORRIES

MY FAVOURITE MOMENT

MY MIND

WHATEVER YOU ARE, BE A GOOD ONE.

DAY 6:_____

MY PLANS

MY GOALS

MY ACHIEVEMENTS

MY WORRIES

MY FAVOURITE MOMENT

MY MIND

DAY 7:_____

MY PLANS

MY GOALS

MY ACHIEVEMENTS

MY WORRIES

MY FAVOURITE MOMENT

MY MIND

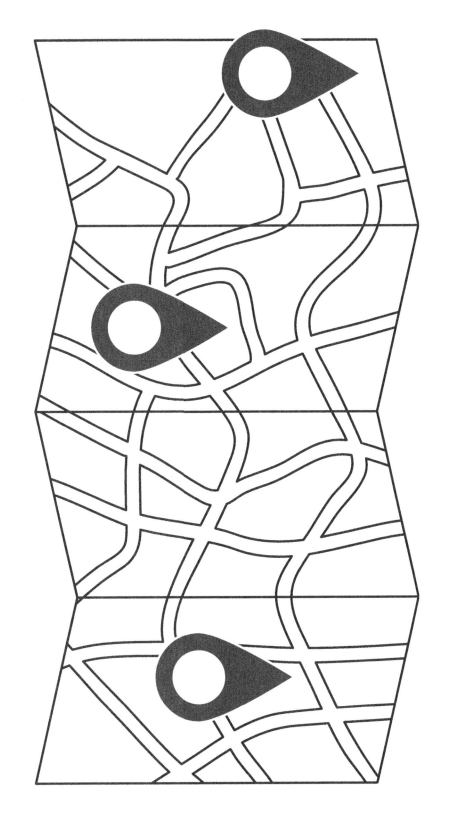

WEEK 11 MIND DUMP

MENTAL HEALTH

WEEK 12 :_____

DAY 1

DAY 2

DAY 3

DAY 4

DAY 5

DAY 6

DAY 7

TOTAL _____

TOTAL _____

TOTAL _____

BEST DAY

MOST DIFFICULT DAY

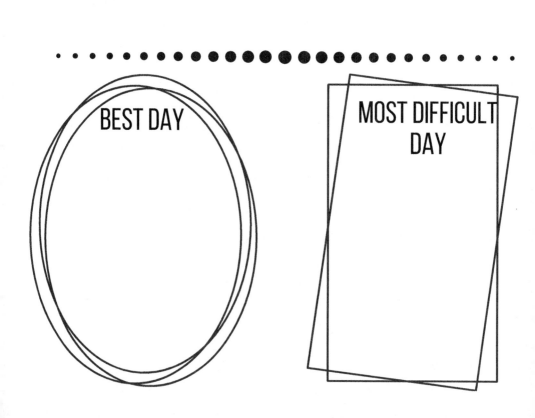

WEEK 12 : _____ HABIT TRACKER

HABIT	GOAL	1	2	3	4	5	6	7	CHANGES TO MAKE

DAY 1:_____

MY PLANS

MY GOALS

MY ACHIEVEMENTS

MY WORRIES

MY FAVOURITE MOMENT

MY MIND

DAY 2:_____

MY PLANS

MY GOALS

MY ACHIEVEMENTS

MY WORRIES

MY FAVOURITE MOMENT

MY MIND

DAY 3:_____

MY PLANS

MY GOALS

MY ACHIEVEMENTS

MY WORRIES

MY FAVOURITE MOMENT

MY MIND

DAY 4:_____

MY PLANS

MY GOALS

MY ACHIEVEMENTS

MY WORRIES

MY FAVOURITE MOMENT

MY MIND

DAY 5:_____

MY PLANS

MY GOALS

MY ACHIEVEMENTS

MY WORRIES

MY FAVOURITE MOMENT

MY MIND

DAY 6:_____

MY PLANS

MY GOALS

MY ACHIEVEMENTS

MY WORRIES

MY FAVOURITE MOMENT

MY MIND

Be brave enough to be bad at something new.

DAY 7:_____

MY PLANS

MY GOALS

MY ACHIEVEMENTS

MY WORRIES

MY FAVOURITE MOMENT

MY MIND

WEEK 12 MIND DUMP

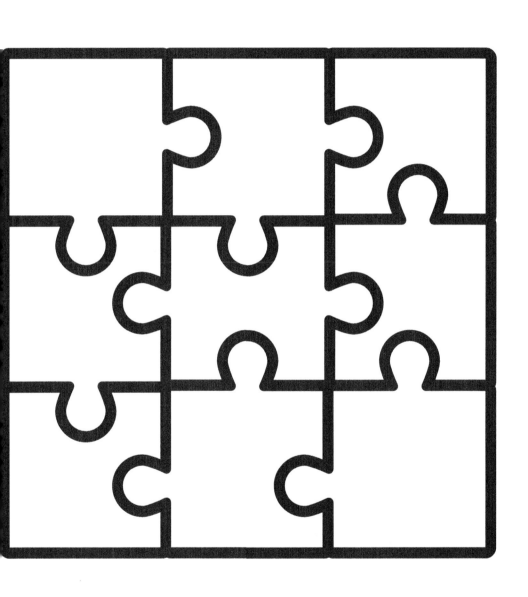

MENTAL HEALTH

WEEK 13 :_____

DAY 1
DAY 2
DAY 3
DAY 4
DAY 5
DAY 6
DAY 7

TOTAL _____

TOTAL _____

TOTAL _____

BEST DAY

MOST DIFFICULT DAY

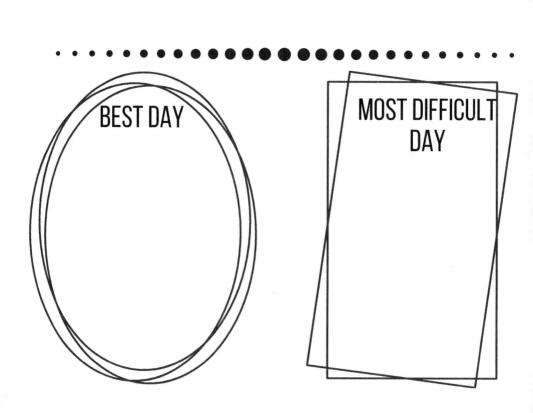

HABIT TRACKER

WEEK 13 : _____

HABIT	GOAL	1	2	3	4	5	6	7	CHANGES TO MAKE

DAY 1:_____

MY PLANS

MY GOALS

MY ACHIEVEMENTS

MY WORRIES

MY FAVOURITE MOMENT

MY MIND

DAY 2:_____

MY PLANS

MY GOALS

MY ACHIEVEMENTS

MY WORRIES

MY FAVOURITE MOMENT

MY MIND

DAY 3:_____

MY PLANS

MY GOALS

MY ACHIEVEMENTS

MY WORRIES

MY FAVOURITE MOMENT

MY MIND

DAY 4:_____

MY PLANS

MY GOALS

MY ACHIEVEMENTS

MY WORRIES

MY FAVOURITE MOMENT

MY MIND

DAY 5:_____

MY PLANS

MY GOALS

MY ACHIEVEMENTS

MY WORRIES

MY FAVOURITE MOMENT

MY MIND

DAY 6:_____

MY PLANS

MY GOALS

MY ACHIEVEMENTS

MY WORRIES

MY FAVOURITE MOMENT

MY MIND

DAY 7:_____

MY PLANS

MY GOALS

MY ACHIEVEMENTS

MY WORRIES

MY FAVOURITE MOMENT

MY MIND

It only
seems
impossible
until it is
done

WEEK 13 MIND DUMP

MENTAL HEALTH

WEEK 14 :_____

DAY 1

DAY 2

DAY 3

DAY 4

DAY 5

DAY 6

DAY 7

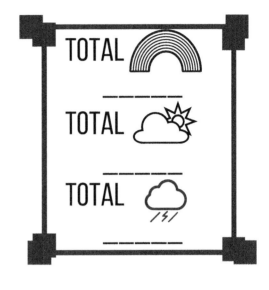

TOTAL

_____

TOTAL

_____

TOTAL

_____

BEST DAY

MOST DIFFICULT DAY

HABIT TRACKER

WEEK 14 : _____

HABIT	GOAL	1	2	3	4	5	6	7	CHANGES TO MAKE

DAY 1:_____

MY PLANS

MY GOALS

MY ACHIEVEMENTS

MY WORRIES

MY FAVOURITE MOMENT

MY MIND

DAY 2:_____

MY PLANS

MY GOALS

MY ACHIEVEMENTS

MY WORRIES

MY FAVOURITE MOMENT

MY MIND

DAY 3:_____

MY PLANS

MY GOALS

MY ACHIEVEMENTS

MY WORRIES

MY FAVOURITE MOMENT

MY MIND

DAY 4:_____

MY PLANS

MY GOALS

MY ACHIEVEMENTS

MY WORRIES

MY FAVOURITE MOMENT

MY MIND

DAY 5:_____

MY PLANS

MY GOALS

MY ACHIEVEMENTS

MY WORRIES

MY FAVOURITE MOMENT

MY MIND

DAY 6:_____

MY PLANS

MY GOALS

MY ACHIEVEMENTS

MY WORRIES

MY FAVOURITE MOMENT

MY MIND

DAY 7:_____

MY PLANS

MY GOALS

MY ACHIEVEMENTS

MY WORRIES

MY FAVOURITE MOMENT

MY MIND

WEEK 14 MIND DUMP

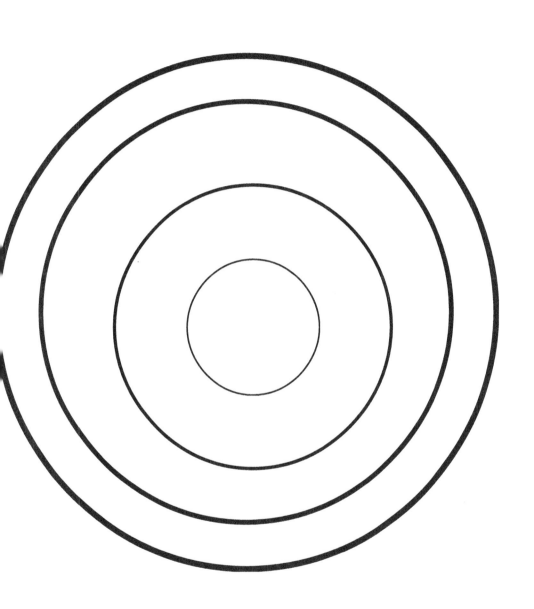

MENTAL HEALTH

WEEK 15 :_____

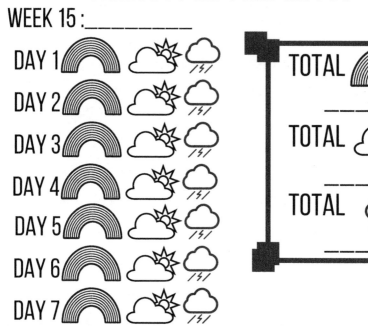

DAY 1

DAY 2

DAY 3

DAY 4

DAY 5

DAY 6

DAY 7

TOTAL

_____

TOTAL

_____

TOTAL

_____

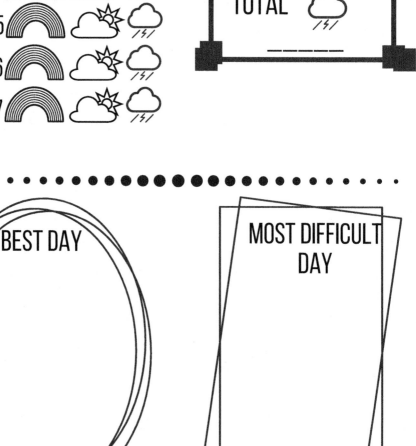

BEST DAY

MOST DIFFICULT DAY

WEEK 15 :_____

HABIT TRACKER

HABIT	GOAL	1	2	3	4	5	6	7	CHANGES TO MAKE

DAY 1:_____

MY PLANS

MY GOALS

MY ACHIEVEMENTS

MY WORRIES

MY FAVOURITE MOMENT

MY MIND

DAY 2:_____

MY PLANS

MY GOALS

MY ACHIEVEMENTS

MY WORRIES

MY FAVOURITE MOMENT

MY MIND

DAY 3:_____

MY PLANS

MY GOALS

MY ACHIEVEMENTS

MY WORRIES

MY FAVOURITE MOMENT

MY MIND

DAY 4:_____

MY PLANS

MY GOALS

MY ACHIEVEMENTS

MY WORRIES

MY FAVOURITE MOMENT

MY MIND

DAY 5:_____

MY PLANS

MY GOALS

MY ACHIEVEMENTS

MY WORRIES

MY FAVOURITE MOMENT

MY MIND

DAY 6: _____

MY PLANS

MY GOALS

MY ACHIEVEMENTS

MY WORRIES

MY FAVOURITE MOMENT

MY MIND

DAY 7:_____

MY PLANS

MY GOALS

MY ACHIEVEMENTS

MY WORRIES

MY FAVOURITE MOMENT

MY MIND

WEEK 15 MIND DUMP

MENTAL HEALTH

WEEK 16 :_____

DAY 1

DAY 2

DAY 3

DAY 4

DAY 5

DAY 6

DAY 7

TOTAL

_____

TOTAL

_____

TOTAL

_____

BEST DAY

MOST DIFFICULT DAY

WEEK 16 : _____

HABIT TRACKER

HABIT	GOAL	1	2	3	4	5	6	7	CHANGES TO MAKE

DAY 1:_____

MY PLANS

MY GOALS

MY ACHIEVEMENTS

MY WORRIES

MY FAVOURITE MOMENT

MY MIND

MAKE YOUR MARK

DAY 2:_____

MY PLANS

MY GOALS

MY ACHIEVEMENTS

MY WORRIES

MY FAVOURITE MOMENT

MY MIND

DAY 3:_____

MY PLANS

MY GOALS

MY ACHIEVEMENTS

MY WORRIES

MY FAVOURITE MOMENT

MY MIND

DAY 4:_____

MY PLANS

MY GOALS

MY ACHIEVEMENTS

MY WORRIES

MY FAVOURITE MOMENT

MY MIND

DAY 5:_____

MY PLANS

MY GOALS

MY ACHIEVEMENTS

MY WORRIES

MY FAVOURITE MOMENT

MY MIND

DAY 6:_____

MY PLANS

MY GOALS

MY ACHIEVEMENTS

MY WORRIES

MY FAVOURITE MOMENT

MY MIND

DAY 7:_____

MY PLANS

MY GOALS

MY ACHIEVEMENTS

MY WORRIES

MY FAVOURITE MOMENT

MY MIND

WEEK 16 MIND DUMP

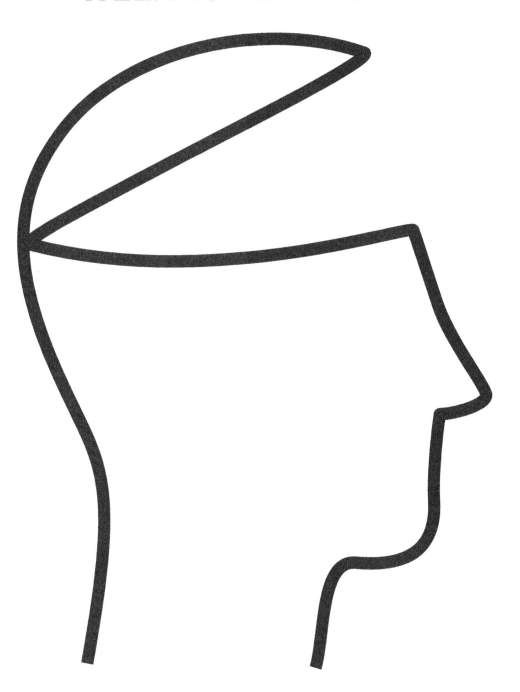

Hello my friend!

Look at you go! You've complete 4 months! That's 16 weeks, 112 days, 2688 hours, 161,280 minutes (woo Maths!).

So what now? Well, just like how you use this journal, what you do now is completely up to you. You may feel like you're ready to go on without a daily guide now. If so, good for you! Maybe you want to get another copy of this journal and keep going for the next four months (thanks, by the way!), or maybe you've got a better idea of how to support yourself and want to create your own. Whatever you decide to do now, know that you have got through the last four months, and you **will** get through the next four, and the next, and the next...I'm sure you can see where I am going with this.

My friend, I think of you as a superhero. Not because you can move faster than the speed of light, or have some crazy gadgets attached to your belt. I know it's cheesy but your super power is the power to keep going, and my word it is the best power to have.

Goodbye my friend.

— *Attila Made*
xx

Printed in Great Britain
by Amazon